PORTRAITS OF THE STATES

★ ★

NEW HAMPSHIRE

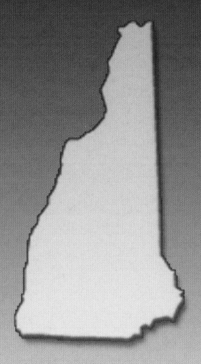

by William David Thomas

GARETH**STEVENS**

A Member of the WRC Media Family of Companies

Please visit our web site at: www.garethstevens.com
For a free color catalog describing Gareth Stevens Publishing's
list of high-quality books and multimedia programs, call
1-800-542-2595 (USA) or 1-800-387-3178 (Canada).
Gareth Stevens Publishing's fax: (877) 542-2596.

Library of Congress Cataloging-in-Publication Data

Thomas, William, 1947-
    New Hampshire / William David Thomas.
      p. cm. — (Portraits of the states)
    Includes bibliographical references and index.
    ISBN-10: 0-8368-4704-0   ISBN-13: 978-0-8368-4704-8 (lib. bdg.)
    ISBN-10: 0-8368-4721-0   ISBN-13: 978-0-8368-4721-5 (softcover)
    1. New Hampshire--Juvenile literature. I. Title. II. Series.
    F34.3T45   2007
    974.2—dc22   2006004072

This edition first published in 2007 by
Gareth Stevens Publishing
A Weekly Reader Company
1 Reader's Digest Rd.
Pleasantville, NY 10570-7000 USA

This edition copyright © 2007 by Gareth Stevens, Inc.

Editorial direction: Mark J. Sachner
Project manager: Jonatha A. Brown
Editor: Catherine Gardner
Art direction and design: Tammy West
Picture research: Diane Laska-Swanke
Indexer: Walter Kronenberg
Production: Jessica Morris and Robert Kraus

Picture credits: Cover, pp. 9, 20 © Paul Rezendes/www.paulrezendes.com;
p. 4 © Gibson Stock Photography; p. 5 © John and Barbara Gerlach/Visuals
Unlimited; p. 6 © Kean Collection/Getty Images; p. 8 © Mansell/Time & Life
Pictures/Getty Images; p. 10 © CORBIS; p. 12 © Steve Liss/Time & Life
Pictures/Getty Images; pp. 15, 21, 27 © BobLegg.com Impact Photography;
p. 16 © Bettmann/CORBIS; p. 17 © David Young-Wolff/PhotoEdit; p. 18
© Nancy Carter/North Wind Picture Archives; p. 22 © Mae Scanlan; p. 24
© John Elk III; p. 25 © AP Images; p. 26 © Tim Seaver; p. 29 © James P. Rowan

Printed in the United States of America

2 3 4 5 6 7 8 9 10 09 08 07

CONTENTS

★ ★

Chapter 1 Introduction......................4

Chapter 2 History.......................6

Time Line 13

Chapter 3 People 14

Chapter 4 The Land.....................18

Chapter 5 Economy......................22

Chapter 6 Government 24

Chapter 7 Things to See and Do 26

Glossary 30

To Find Out More.................31

Index 32

Words that are defined in the Glossary appear
in **bold** the first time they are used in the text.

On the Cover: This is the beautiful Mount Washington Hotel.
Behind it is the snow-covered mountain for which it was named.

Introduction

New Hampshire is a small state with a long history. It was one of the first thirteen states of the United States. It was once a state of forests and small farms. As the years passed, New Hampshire became famous for its factories. Today, it is home to computer and Internet businesses.

New Hampshire is also a state of great beauty. Its lakes, rivers, and mountains are a joy for people who like to hike, ski, and fish. Visitors come to see the state's lovely small towns, covered bridges, and beautiful autumn leaves.

See for yourself. Visit the cities, towns, mountains, and lakes. Meet the people. Get to know New Hampshire!

A family enjoys the fall colors as they fish from a canoe on Echo Lake.

The state flag of New Hampshire.

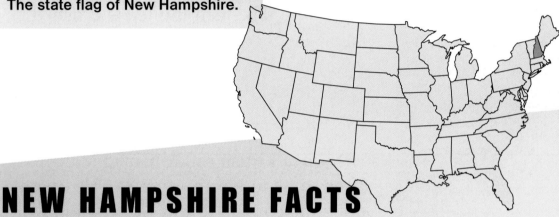

NEW HAMPSHIRE FACTS

- Became the 9th U.S. State: June 21, 1788
- Population (2006): 1,314,895
- Capital: Concord
- Biggest Cities: Manchester, Nashua, Concord, Rochester
- Size: 8,968 square miles (23,227 square kilometers)
- Nickname: The Granite State
- State Tree: White birch
- State Flower: Pink lady's slipper
- State Animal: White-tailed deer
- State Bird: Purple finch

History

Native American people were settled in New Hampshire five hundred years ago. Two groups of Native people were the Abenaki and the Pennacook. These people built dome-shaped homes called **wigwams**. The men hunted and fished. The women cared for gardens of squash, corn, and beans. They cooked sap from maple trees to make syrup and sugar.

The First Europeans

In 1603, a British sailor named Martin Pring came to North America. He sailed along the coast. He was the first known white man to visit New Hampshire. Other explorers from France and Britain came to this area in the early 1600s. They drew maps, but did not stay long. British settlers came to a place called Odiorne's Point in 1623. These settlers stayed only a few years.

In 1622, the British king gave a large piece of

British settlers bring supplies ashore at Odiorne's Point. They landed here in 1623.

land to two men. They later divided it. One of the men, named John Mason, came from Hampshire, in Britain. He called his land New Hampshire. He sent people to live there. By 1631, they had settled near the coast. Lots of wild strawberries grew there, so the settlers named the area Strawbery Banke. Later, it would be called Portsmouth.

In time, more villages were built. They became part of the Massachusetts

Famous People of New Hampshire

Sarah Josepha Hale

Born: October 24, 1788, Newport, New Hampshire

Died: April 30, 1879, Philadelphia, Pennsylvania

Sarah Hale taught herself to be a writer. She wrote the nursery rhyme "Mary Had a Little Lamb." She wrote books and poetry, too. Later, Hale was in charge of a well-known magazine for women. It was called *Godey's Ladies Book*. She often wrote about starting a new holiday. She wanted a day when people in the United States would give thanks. Hale finally got her wish. President Abraham Lincoln made Thanksgiving a holiday in 1863.

FUN FACTS

A Cloud of Fire

Four hundred years ago, Passaconaway was a chief of the Pennacook tribe. He was said to be a great magician. When settlers from Britain came, he helped keep peace between them and his people. A legend says that when he died, his body was put on a sled. Wolves pulled it to the top of Mount Washington. There, it disappeared in a cloud of fire.

Bay **Colony**. But the settlers did not like the colony's laws. They wanted to have their own governor. Finally, in 1741, the colony of New Hampshire was formed. It belonged to the British king.

Meanwhile, the settlers started farms. They used trees from the forests to

In the early 1770s, crowds of American colonists raged against British taxes. They thought the taxes were unfair.

build their homes and barns. The trees were used to build ships, too. New Hampshire became an important center for building ships.

Native Americans did not like these changes. Their fields and hunting lands were being taken over by whites. Before long, the two groups began fighting. Many Natives were killed. Others died of the diseases brought by the whites. Still others moved to Canada. By 1763, few Natives were left in New Hampshire.

Many people come to New Hampshire to see the state's famous covered bridges. This one was built in 1864.

A War for Independence

In the mid-1700s, the British king needed money. Laws were passed that made the colonists pay high taxes. They could not vote on these new taxes or any other laws. This made them angry.

People in New Hampshire and the other colonies began to talk about being free from Britain. In 1774, a group of men from New Hampshire attacked a British fort near Portsmouth. Britain and the colonies were soon at war.

New Hampshire built ships for the navy. It sent soldiers to fight for freedom.

FUN FACTS

Kissing Bridges

New Hampshire is famous for its covered bridges. They are wooden bridges covered by a roof and walls. The cover kept snow off the bridges in winter. They were also called "kissing bridges." Years ago, young couples went inside the bridges. There, they could kiss without being seen.

In 1776, New Hampshire declared its freedom from Britain. It was one of the first colonies to do so. The colonists fought the British in the Revolutionary War. In 1783, the British lost the war, and the colonies were free. On June 21, 1788, New Hampshire became the ninth state of a new nation. It was the United States.

Factories and Cities

New Hampshire's mountains had many rivers. The rivers' fast-moving water could be used to power machinery. In 1804, a cotton mill was built in New Ipswich. Soon, more factories were built along the state's rivers. People moved to these areas for jobs. Towns and

IN NEW HAMPSHIRE'S HISTORY

Manchester's Mills

Manchester was once a small village on the Merrimack River. In 1810, the Amoskeag Company bought a small textile mill there. Later, it began to build more mills. Manchester began to grow. By 1920, the Amoskeag Mills were the biggest textile mills in the world. Thousands of people worked there. Then **labor strikes** and the **Great Depression** hurt the company. The mills closed in 1936. Today, some of the old buildings are open again. Computer companies, restaurants, and museums use the space where cloth was once made.

Workers go home after a long day in the Amoskeag cloth mills. Long ago, children worked in the mills along with their parents.

cities began to grow around the factories. Wagons and shoes were made in some of the factories, but most of them made cloth. New Hampshire became a world leader in making **textiles**.

The state's mountains and hills also had lots of granite. Granite is a kind of rock. It is very strong and good for building. The state became known as the Granite State.

The factories in New Hampshire made cloth and other goods for more than one hundred years. During this time, the Portsmouth naval yard built submarines and ships for the U.S. Navy. After World War II ended, in 1945, these businesses began to die out.

Change and Growth

New businesses started in New Hampshire. They made tools, parts for airplanes, and computers. People came to the state for jobs in the new companies. The **population** of the state began to grow. But change and growth are not always easy. They can cause problems.

In the 1970s, the state needed more electricity. A company wanted to build a **nuclear power** plant near

IN NEW HAMPSHIRE'S HISTORY

The Presidential Primaries
Every four years, New Hampshire plays a big role in U.S. politics. The people who want to be president of the United States come to the state. They talk about their ideas with the people. Then, a primary election is held. This election shows which **candidate** in each party is liked the most and might make a good candidate for president. Primaries like this are held in many U.S. states. The primary in New Hampshire is important because it is first.

The Seabrook Nuclear Power Plant provides 7 percent of the electricity used in New England.

Seabrook. Some people thought nuclear power was dangerous. Others said it would hurt the environment. Many people fought against the plant. Hundreds of them were arrested. But the plant was built. It opened in 1990.

As more people came, the state needed more money for schools. Lawmakers wanted to start an **income tax**. This is a tax on money earned by working. Most other states have a tax like this. New Hampshire never did. The state's people and lawmakers argued about the income tax

for almost ten years. It was defeated in 1999.

The people of this state love their freedom. Today, as in the past, they stand up for what they believe.

FUN FACTS

Golf on the Moon
Alan Shepard was born and raised in New Hampshire. He became a navy pilot, then an astronaut. In 1971, he went to the moon. Shepard secretly carried a golf club and some golf balls with him. He is the only person (so far) ever to hit a golf ball on the moon.

★ ★ ★ Time Line ★ ★ ★

1500	Native Americans live in villages near New Hampshire's coast.
1622	John Mason is given land by the king of Britain. He later names his land New Hampshire.
1631	Settlers start the town of Strawbery Banke, now called Portsmouth.
1741	The colony of New Hampshire is formed.
1776	New Hampshire declares independence from Britain.
1788	New Hampshire becomes the ninth U.S. state.
1804	The state's first cotton mill is built in New Ipswich.
1936	The Amoskeag Mills close.
1977	Fourteen hundred people are arrested for protesting the building of the Seabrook Nuclear Power Plant.
1986	Teacher Christa McAuliffe dies when the space shuttle *Challenger* blows up.
1999	A state income tax bill is defeated.
2003	The Old Man of the Mountain falls down.

People

New Hampshire's population is small, but it is growing. People come to the state because new businesses are starting there. People also come because New Hampshire has a high "quality of life." That means there is not much crime, houses do not cost too much, and taxes are not too high. It also means there are good schools, good hospitals, and lots of things to do.

About half of New Hampshire's people live in cities. The largest cities, such as

Hispanics
This chart shows the different racial backgrounds of people in New Hampshire. In the 2000 U.S. Census, 1.7 percent of the people in New Hampshire called themselves Latino or Hispanic. Most of them or their relatives came from places where Spanish is spoken. Hispanics do not appear on this chart because they may come from any racial background.

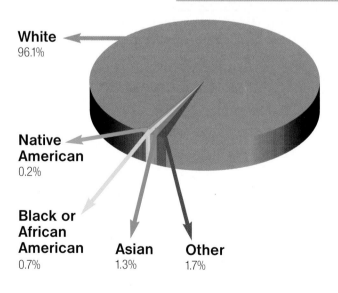

The People of New Hampshire

Total Population 1,314,895

White
96.1%

Native
American
0.2%

Black or
African
American
0.7%

Asian
1.3%

Other
1.7%

Percentages are based on the 2000 Census.

14

Nashua and Manchester, are in the southern part of the state. The northern part of the state has smaller towns and fewer people.

People from Many Places

Most of the early white settlers in New Hampshire came from Britain. In the 1800s, **immigrants** began to come from other countries. They came from Portugal, Poland, Ireland, and Greece. Lots of people came from Canada, too. Most of the people from Canada were French Canadians. They came from the province of Quebec. In recent years, people have come to the state from India and Korea.

Religion

Most of the white settlers who came from Britain were Protestants. Today, New Hampshire has many Methodist, Baptist and other Protestant churches. The

Famous People of New Hampshire

Christa McAuliffe

Born: September 2, 1948, Framingham, Massachusetts

Died: January 28, 1986, Cape Canaveral, Florida

Christa McAuliffe was a social studies teacher in Concord. In 1984, she learned about a program to send a teacher into space. She applied and was chosen from thousands of other teachers. She said her space journey would be "the ultimate field trip." But it was not to be. The space shuttle *Challenger* exploded just seconds after it took off. McAuliffe and the six other crew members died in the explosion. A planetarium and science museum was built in her honor in Concord. A marker at her high school has her words: "I touch the future — I teach."

This is Christa McAuliffe wearing her NASA astronaut's uniform. She was chosen to be the first teacher in space. She died when the Space Shuttle *Challenger* blew up just after take off.

state has meeting houses for Quakers, too.

French Canadians who came to this area brought the Roman Catholic faith with them. Today in New Hampshire, about one person in three is Catholic.

Jews, Muslims, and people of other faiths also live here.

Education

There have been public schools in New Hampshire for more than three hundred years. An early law said that reading and writing had to be taught in any town with fifty or more families. The first public high school in the United States opened in Portsmouth in 1830. Once, each town or district in the state ran its own schools. Today, all public schools are controlled by the State Board of Education.

New Hampshire's people are some of the best educated in the country.

Almost nine out of every ten adults in the state have finished high school. Many of these people have gone to college, too.

The state has about thirty colleges and universities. One of the largest of them is the University of New Hampshire, in Durham. More than ten thousand students go to classes there. Dartmouth College is one of the oldest colleges in the country. It started in Hanover in 1769.

A clock tower rises above the trees on the campus of Dartmouth College in Hanover.

The Land

The land that is now New Hampshire was formed millions of years ago by **glaciers**. The glaciers made the state's mountains, valleys, and lakes. The state is in a part of the country called New England. This is a group of six northeastern states that were settled mainly by people from England.

Climate

New Hampshire has four different seasons. Winter is very cold, with plenty of snow. Spring is cool and may be wet. Summer is fairly short and mild. Fall is a beautiful season. The leaves on the trees turn bright red, orange, and yellow. Lots of people come to see them.

Two loons swim past bright fall colors on the Androscoggin River.

NEW HAMPSHIRE

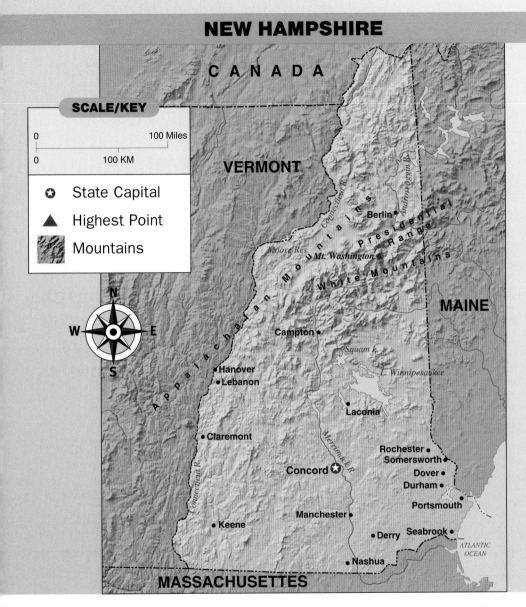

CANADA

SCALE/KEY

0 _____ 100 Miles

0 _____ 100 KM

⊛ State Capital

▲ Highest Point

▨ Mountains

VERMONT

N
W · E
S

Connecticut R.

Berlin

Androscoggin R.

Presidential Range

Appalachian Mountains

Moore Res. Mt. Washington ▲

White Mountains

MAINE

Campton

Squam L.

Hanover
Lebanon

L. Winnipesaukee

Laconia

Claremont

Merrimack R.

Rochester
Somersworth
Dover
Durham

Connecticut R.

Concord ⊛

Portsmouth

Keene

Manchester

Derry Seabrook

ATLANTIC
OCEAN

Nashua

MASSACHUSETTES

The Atlantic Coast

A small part of this state touches the Atlantic Ocean. The Atlantic coastline is just 18 miles (29 km) long. The land in this part of the state is mostly flat. Seabirds such as gulls and terns fly overhead. There are sandy beaches for swimming. The city of Portsmouth is near the coast.

19

The Upland

Between the coast and the mountains is the Upland. The state's famous granite is found here. Hills, lakes, and forests cover the land. Deer and fox live among the birch, oak, pine, and maple trees. Beaver and mink live near the streams. Colorful daisies, violets, and other wildflowers bloom in the meadows in the Upland.

The Merrimack River winds through the Upland. Some of the state's largest cities, such as Manchester, were built along its banks. Part of the Upland is called the Lakes Region. This area

Major Rivers
Connecticut River   407 miles (655 km) long
Androscoggin River   157 miles (253 km) long
Merrimack River   110 miles (177 km) long

has more than two hundred lakes. Lake Winnipesaukee is the biggest. The region is very popular with **tourists**.

The White Mountains

The White Mountains cover the central and northern parts of New Hampshire. Their name may come from

Thick forests cover much of the White Mountains. Many different kinds of animals live in this wild area.

the snow that covers their tops for much of the year. The highest peaks form the Presidential Range. They are named for U.S. presidents. At 6,288 feet (1,917 meters), Mount Washington is the state's tallest mountain. Fir and spruce trees grow in the lower parts of these mountains. Deer, rabbits, and squirrels live there. In summer, hikers often find wild blueberries growing in sunny places.

The far northern part of New Hampshire borders Canada. This area is called the "North Country" or the "Great North Woods." Few people live here. Timber companies own much of the heavily forested land. The forests are home to moose and bears. Sportsmen come to the area to hunt or to fish for trout and salmon.

FACTS

Windy Weather
A weather station sits at the top of Mount Washington. In 1934, workers there measured a terrible gust of wind. The wind speed was 231 miles (372 km) per hour.

These rocks looked like a face on the side of a cliff. The face was called the Old Man of the Mountain. It was a famous sight. But now the Old Man is gone. The rocks fell down in 2003.

Economy

New Hampshire began as a farming state. The people there raised fruit, vegetables, and cattle. Mining and logging were important, too. Later, cloth made in mills was the top product.

Milk is now New Hampshire's biggest farm product. Some granite is still mined in the state, too. Loggers still cut trees for lumber and to make paper. But the textile mills are gone.

Computers, Televisions, and Technology

Today, New Hampshire turns out many **high-tech** products. Some factories in the state make aircraft parts. Others make

Tourists board a sight-seeing ship for a ride on Lake Winnipesaukee.

special tools and equipment for doctors and scientists. Still others make television sets and computers.

Many Internet companies have come to the state, too. Most of these companies are in cities and towns near the Atlantic coast. The seacoast has so many electronic and high-tech businesses that it is nicknamed "the e-coast."

Tourism

Tourism is a big business in New Hampshire. The state's mountains, lakes, and parks attract lots of visitors each year. These visitors make jobs for many people. Hotel and restaurant workers are part of the tourist business. Workers at ski centers and campgrounds serve visitors to the state, too.

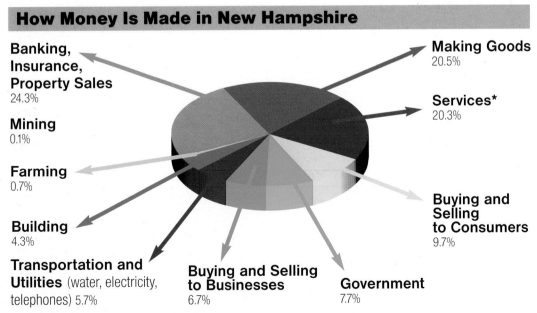

How Money Is Made in New Hampshire

Banking, Insurance, Property Sales 24.3%

Mining 0.1%

Farming 0.7%

Building 4.3%

Transportation and Utilities (water, electricity, telephones) 5.7%

Buying and Selling to Businesses 6.7%

Government 7.7%

Making Goods 20.5%

Services* 20.3%

Buying and Selling to Consumers 9.7%

* Services include jobs in hotels, restaurants, auto repair, medicine, teaching, and entertainment.

Government

New Hampshire's state government is like the government of the United States. It has three parts, or branches.

Executive Branch

The executive branch carries out the laws of the state. It is led by the governor. The governor is helped by five people who form the Executive Council.

Legislative Branch

The legislative branch makes the laws for the state. In New Hampshire,

This is the State House in Concord. New Hampshire's government has met here since 1819.

More people take part in the government of New Hampshire than in any other state. Here, the state Senate is holding a meeting in the State House.

this branch is called the General Court. It has two parts. These parts are the Senate and the House of Representatives. There are four hundred representatives in the House. That is far more than any other state.

Judicial Branch

Courts and judges make up the state's judicial branch.

They may decide whether a person who is accused of committing a crime is guilty.

Local Government

Most cities are run by a city manager or mayor. Towns are run by a group of people called selectmen. Each town holds a meeting at least once a year. Any adult in town may speak at this meeting and help make decisions that affect the whole town.

NEW HAMPSHIRE'S STATE GOVERNMENT

Executive		Legislative		Judicial	
Office	**Length of Term**	**Body**	**Length of Term**	**Court**	**Length of Term**
Governor	2 years	Senate (24 members)	2 years	Supreme (5 justices)	Until age 70
Executive Council	2 years	House of Representatives (400 members)	2 years	Superior (26 judges)	Until age 70

25

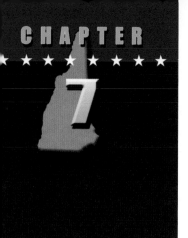

Things to See and Do

New Hampshire may be small, but it offers lots of things to see and do. You can enjoy history, fun festivals, and the great outdoors.

History Comes Alive

Concord is home to the Museum of New Hampshire History. It shows happenings in the state from the Native Americans to modern times.

You can see history come to life at the Strawbery Banke Museum in Portsmouth. This **restored** village shows how people lived and worked in New Hampshire more than two hundred years ago. While you

Hikers climb New Hampshire's mountains even in winter. The big pile of stones is called a cairn. It marks the trail to the top.

are in Portsmouth, be sure to visit the harbor. You can tour fishing boats or take a whale-watching boat trip.

Wakefield has a museum that is all about children. The Museum of Childhood has a one-room schoolhouse from the 1890s, dolls, teddy bears, trains, and more.

Fun for All

Several towns in New Hampshire hold First Night celebrations on New Year's Eve. Folks enjoy ice carving contests, food, and fireworks.

Do you like seafood? Then you might like to visit Portsmouth for the Chowderfest. You can try all sorts of clam and fish chowder.

Hot air balloons float over the Suncook River on a warm summer day. Many towns in New Hampshire hold balloon festivals each year in the summer.

27

Famous People of New Hampshire

Robert Frost

Born: March 26, 1874, San Francisco, California

Died: January 29, 1963, Boston, Massachusetts

Robert Frost was one of the most famous poets in the United States. His family moved to New Hampshire when Frost was a boy. He spent many years in the small town of Franconia. There, he farmed, raised his family, and wrote. Many of his poems are about country life in New Hampshire. One of his most famous poems is called, "Stopping by Woods on a Snowy Evening." In 1961, Frost wrote a special poem for John F. Kennedy. He read it at the ceremony when Kennedy was sworn in as president of the United States.

In autumn, Warner has a Fall Foliage Festival. You can see a country fair, oxen pulls, and road race. It even has a pie-eating contest!

If you like the music of fiddles and guitars, come to Campton. The Pemi Valley Bluegrass Festival has lots of foot-tapping music.

Outdoor Fun

New Hampshire's lakes and mountains are great. Lake Winnipesaukee is the state's largest lake. It is a popular spot for swimming, boating, and fishing. In Wolfeboro, a walking path takes you past rushing waterfalls. Another fun place is White Mountain National Forest. It is in the northern part of the state. There, you can hike, fish, and camp. In the southern part of the state is Mount Monadnock. People say that it has been climbed

Famous People of New Hampshire

Carlton Fisk

Born: December 26, 1947, Bellows Falls, Vermont

As a boy, Carlton Fisk lived in Charlestown, New Hampshire. He played major league baseball for more than twenty years. He played more games as a catcher than any player in history. Fisk was known as "the catcher who changed socks." He played first for the Boston Red Sox. Later, he played for the Chicago White Sox. In 2000, he was voted into the Baseball Hall of Fame.

At the top of Mount Washington, you can visit a museum and take a tour of this weather station.

more times than any other mountain in North America.

Things do not slow down in winter. A dog sled race is a favorite event in Laconia. The teams go right through the town's streets. You can go skiing or snowboarding at places around the state. Did you ever try snowshoes? Or ride a snowmobile? New Hampshire is the place for these winter sports!

Sports

Lots of sports fans follow New Hampshire's college football and basketball teams. There are no major **professional** sports teams in the state. Many fans cheer for the pro teams in Boston, the nearest large city.

GLOSSARY

★ ★

candidate — a person trying to get elected to a political office such as mayor or president

colony — a group of people living in a new land that is controlled by the place they came from

glaciers — huge, thick masses of ice that move slowly across the land

Great Depression — a time, in the 1930s, when many people lost jobs and businesses lost money

high-tech — having to do with computers and other advanced machines

immigrants — people who leave one country to live in another country

income tax — a tax paid on money earned by working or investing

labor strikes — plans by workers to refuse to work until they get better pay or working conditions

nuclear power — a very advanced type of power first used in the mid-1900s

population — the number of people who live in a place, such as a city or state

professional — earning money for doing an activity

restored — repaired so something is like new

textiles — cloth, usually made with machinery

tourists — people who travel for fun

wigwams — small, dome-shaped homes that were built by Native Americans and were made from bark, sticks, and furs

Books

Christa McAuliffe: Teacher in Space. Corinne Naden and Rose Blue (Millbrook Press)

The Legend of the Old Man of the Mountain. Denise Ortakales (Sleeping Bear Press)

New Hampshire. From Sea to Shining Sea (series). Terry Miller Shannon (Children's Press)

New Hampshire. Hello U.S.A. (series). Dottie Brown (Lerner).

New Hampshire. Rookie Read-About Geography (series). Simone T. Ribke (Children's Press)

The New Hampshire Colony. Colonies (series). Bob Italia (Checkerboard Books)

Web Sites

Enchanted Learning: New Hampshire
www.enchantedlearning.com/usa/states/newhampshire/

KidSpace
www.ipl.org/div/kidspace/stateknow/nh1.html

New Hampshire Historical Society
www.nhhistory.org/edu/support/slidesindex.htm

New Hampshire: Just For Kids
www.nh.gov/nhfacts/

Abenaki people 6
African Americans 14
Amoskeag Company 10
Androscoggin River
   18, 20
Asian Americans 14
Atlantic Ocean 19

cairns 26
Campton 28
Canada 8, 15, 21
Challenger
   (space shuttle) 16
Charlestown 29
climate 18
Concord 5, 16, 24, 26
Connecticut River 20
covered bridges 9

Dartmouth College 17
Durham 17

Echo Lake 4
education 17

Fisk, Carlton 29
French Canadians 15, 16
Frost, Robert 28

glaciers 18
granite 11, 20, 22
Great Britain 6–10, 15
Great Depression 10
Great North Woods 21

Hale, Sarah Josepha 7
Hanover 17
high-tech products
   22–23
Hispanics 14

Jones, John Paul 8

Laconia 29
Lakes Region 20
Lake Winnipesaukee
   20, 22, 28
Lincoln, Abraham 7

Manchester 5, 10, 15, 20
Mason, John 7
Massachusetts
   Bay Colony 7–8
McAuliffe, Christa 13, 16
Merrimack River
   10, 15, 20
Mount Monadnock
   28–29
Mount Washington
   7, 21, 29
museums 26–27
Mystery Hill 18

Nashua 5, 15
Native Americans
   6–8, 14, 26
New England 12, 18
Newport 7

North Country 21
North Salem 18
nuclear power 11–12

Passaconaway
   (Indian chief) 7
Pennacook people 6, 7
Portsmouth 7–9, 11,
   17, 19, 26–27
presidential primaries 11
Presidential Range 21
Pring, Martin 6

religion 15–17
Revolutionary War 8–10
rivers 10, 20

Shepard, Alan 12
shipbuilding 8, 11
space program 12, 16
sports 29
Strawbery Banke 7

taxes 9, 12, 14
textiles 10, 11, 22
Thanksgiving 7
tourism 20, 22, 23

Wakefield 27
Warner 28
weather 18, 29
White Mountains 20–21
Wolfeboro 28
World War II 11